Vincent van Gogh
빈센트 반 고흐

Biography Comic
who? ㉑ Vincent van Gogh

초판 1쇄 인쇄 2011년 4월 8일
초판 1쇄 발행 2011년 4월 15일

지은이 오영석
그린이 스튜디오 청비
번역 샐리 박
감수 김수희
펴낸이 김선식

Chief Story Creator 김정미
Story Creator 채정은
Design Creator 김경민
Marketing Creator 신문수

Brand Creative Story Team 김정미, 채정은, 박혜연
Creative Design Dept. 최부돈, 황정민, 김태수, 조혜상, 이성희, 김경민
Creative Marketing Dept. 모계영, 이주화, 김하늘, 신문수
　　　　　Communication Team 서선행, 김선준, 박혜원, 전아름
　　　　　Contents Rights Team 이정순, 김미영
New Business Team 우재오
Creative Management Team 김성자, 김미현, 김유미, 정연주, 서여주, 권송이
Outsourcing 임나윤

펴낸곳 (주)다산북스
주소 서울시 마포구 서교동 395-27번지
전화 02-702-1724(기획편집) 02-703-1725(마케팅) 02-704-1724(경영지원)
팩스 02-703-2219
이메일 dasanbooks@hanmail.net
홈페이지 www.dasanbooks.com
출판등록 2005년 12월 23일 제313-2005-00277호

필름 출력 스크린그래픽센타 **종이** 월드페이퍼(주) **인쇄·제본** (주)현문

ISBN 978-89-6370-449-4　14740
SET　978-89-6370-438-8

who?
Vincent van Gogh
빈센트 반 고흐

글 **오영석** | 그림 **스튜디오 청비** | 번역 **샐리 박** | 감수 **김수희**

Dasan Kid

Vincent van Gogh

Dutch painter, March 30, 1853 ~ July 29, 1890

Vincent van Gogh was born in 1853 in a small town called Zundert in the Netherlands. He was the oldest of six children and had a special relationship with his younger brother, Theo.

Due to their family's tight financial situation, Vincent had to work at an early age and found a job in the Hague at an art gallery. He encountered many works of art there and developed an artistic eye, and decided that he wanted to become an artist himself.

As he worked in many different places, he decided that art was not his destiny and headed to Amsterdam to become a minister. However, it was not easy to become a minister. Eventually, he gave up becoming a clergyman and just worked for the church. But the church leaders thought that he brought down the dignity of the church and laid him off. After getting rejected from everything he wanted to do, Vincent was dejected. But instead of giving up, he decided to pursue art once more.

At the age of 27, he was getting a late start in learning art, but he worked harder than anyone else. With his brother, Theo's help, van Gogh was able to move to Paris. He was then able to create his own style with influence from a Japanese printing named *Ukiyo-e*, which used bright colors and impressionists who were able to skillfully portray light.

Van Gogh liked to paint the bright and dazzling sun so he moved down south with his fellow painter friend named Gauguin to a city called Arles. There he painted works such as the *Sunflower series* and *Starry Night*. But not long afterwards, Gauguin left and van Gogh suffered from loneliness and became mentally unstable. He was institutionalized but continued to paint while in hospital. It was there that he sold his first piece, even while his mind was deteriorating. Eventually, van Gogh committed suicide in the very field which he drew as the background in his works.

Vincent van Gogh, the passionate artist, painted over 800 paintings and 1,000 sketches during a period of ten years. Currently, his works are loved by many and just one of his works alone is worth hundreds of millions of dollars.

빈센트 반 고흐

네덜란드의 화가, 1853년 3월 30일 ~ 1890년 7월 29일

빈센트 반 고흐는 1853년, 네덜란드의 작은 마을 준데르트에서 태어났습니다. 6남매 중 첫째였던 그는 4살 어린 동생 테오와 남다른 형제애를 나누며 어린 시절을 보냅니다.

어려운 집안 형편으로 일찍부터 일을 해야 했던 빈센트는 헤이그에 있는 구필 화랑에 취직을 합니다. 이곳에서 더 많은 작품을 접하고 그림을 보는 눈을 키우며 자신도 그림을 그리고 싶다는 생각을 하게 됩니다.

많은 일을 겪으면서 그림이 자신의 길이 아니라고 생각한 빈센트는 목사가 되기 위해 암스테르담으로 갑니다. 그러나 목사가 되는 일도 쉽지는 않았습니다. 결국 그는 목사를 포기하고 전도사가 되지만 교회의 품격을 떨어뜨렸다는 이유로 전도사직에서 해고당합니다. 자신이 원하던 모든 일에서 거부당한 빈센트는 실의에 빠졌습니다. 그러나 그는 포기하지 않고, 자신의 꿈이었던 화가에 다시 도전하기로 합니다.

27살이라는 늦은 나이에 그림 배우기를 시작한 빈센트는 누구보다 열심히 그림을 그립니다. 동생 테오의 도움으로 파리에 살게 된 후로는 화려한 색감의 일본 판화 우키요에와 빛을 표현하는 화풍을 가진 인상파 화가들의 영향을 받아 자신만의 스타일을 창조하기에 이릅니다.

언제나 화려하고 정열적인 햇볕을 그리고 싶어 했던 빈센트는 프랑스 남쪽 지방에 있는 도시 아를로 떠나 친구인 화가 고갱과 함께 생활하며 '해바라기 연작' '별이 빛나는 밤' 등의 작품을 그립니다. 그러나 머지않아 고갱은 떠나 버리고, 외로움에 시달리던 빈센트는 정신병에 걸리고 맙니다. 그는 정신 병원에서도 작품 활동을 계속하였습니다. 그곳에서 처음으로 자신의 작품을 팔게 되었으나, 이미 빈센트의 정신은 피폐해져 있었습니다. 결국, 자신의 작품의 배경이 되었던 밀밭에서 권총 자살로 생을 마감합니다.

열정적인 화가였던 빈센트 반 고흐는 10년간 800여 점의 유화와 1,000점이 넘는 스케치를 남겼습니다. 현재 그의 작품은 한 점에 수백억 원을 호가하며 많은 사람들의 사랑을 받고 있습니다.

이 책을 만든 사람들

글 · 오영석

어린이들이 재미있고 신나게 읽을 수 있는 책을 쓰기 위해 노력하는 작가입니다. 나와 똑같이 고민하고, 실패했던 위인들의 이야기를 통해 독자들도 '할 수 있다'는 마음을 가지길 바랍니다. 작품으로『세계사 한국사』,『과학 교과 주제 탐구Q 몸』,『걸어서 세계 속으로 2. 일본』등이 있습니다.

그림 · 스튜디오 청비

어린이들을 위해 새롭고, 재미있고, 즐거운 이야깃거리를 만드는 만화 창작 집단입니다. 세상을 바꾼 인물들의 삶을 통해 어린이들이 희망찬 미래를 만들어가길 바랍니다. 작품으로『지식 똑똑 경제 리더십 탐구-긍정의 힘』,『why? 서양 근대 사회의 시작』,『why? 세계대전과 전후의 세계』등이 있습니다. 이 책은 이준형 작가님이 그림을 그리셨습니다.

번역 · 샐리 박(Sally Park)

캐나다 토론토에서 태어나고 미국 뉴저주에서 자랐습니다. 유치원부터 중학교까지 한글 학교를 다니고 졸업했습니다. 현재 뉴저지 주립대학교인 럿거스에서 영어와 심리학을 전공하고 있으며, 어린이책을 번역하고 있습니다.

감수 · 김수희

연세대학교에서 역사를 전공했습니다. 이후 한국뿐 아니라 일본, 미국에서 한국어, 일본어, 영어를 가르쳐 왔으며 부모를 위한 영어교육용 책을 썼습니다. 영어교육채널 EBSe '엄마표 영어특강'에서 강의를 하며 홈스쿨, 알파벳과 파닉스, 다차원 테마 영어 수업 기법을 알리고 있습니다. 전국 각지에서 어린이 영어 교육에 대한 강연을 하며 창의적이고 열정적인 교수법으로 영어를 배우고자 하는 어린이와 부모들에게 많은 도움을 주고 있습니다.

Vincent van Gogh

Which of the following is not one of Vincent van Gogh's paintings?

a. *The Potato Eaters*
b. *Starry Night*
c. *Sunrise*

Answer: b

Contents

01 The Boy Who Works at the Gallery

CD1 Track 01 ▶

March 30, 1853.
A baby boy's cries were heard in Zundert, which is a small village in the Netherlands.

Okay, I'll be there soon!

Pastor, the child has been born. Hurry, come with me!

WAAAH WAAAH

Honey!

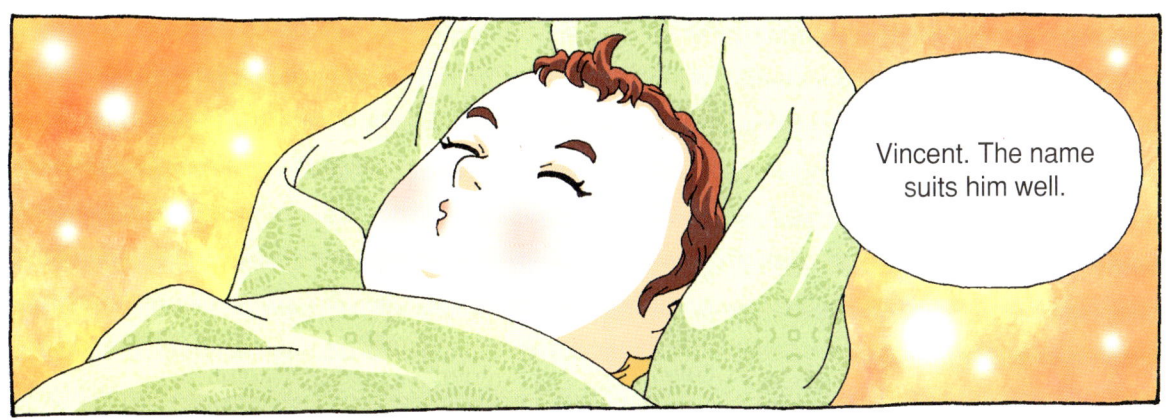

Aw, that's too bad. I was thinking about going to the stream tomorrow to catch some fish!

I'm all better now. It doesn't hurt at all!

Haha, oh really? So that means you won't cry anymore, right?

Ooh, a butterfly.

Ooh.

Vincent, catch the butterfly for me.

Okay! Hold on tight.

I'm running!

14

Oh no,
it's getting away!
Run a little faster!

Vincent liked to draw so whenever he had free time, he would do just that.

PLOP

Theo!

Vincent, stop drawing pictures of fish and come play with me.

I'm almost done. Hold on.

Sheesh, the fish you draw look weird. These fish look so different from the fish that other people draw.

Come here and look closely. Look, look. Don't the fish in this picture look exactly like the ones in the water?

No, the ones you drew have so many layers.

Of course they do. It's because I drew a picture of them swimming. This is what fish look like when they're in motion.

Hmm, I guess I can see what you're saying.

16

Finished! What do you think, Theo?

Wow, it looks like the fish are alive! Awesome.

Hehe. You're the best! Everyone else says my drawings aren't that good.

16-year-old Vincent, who was about to graduate from school, began to worry about his future.

Our Father, who art in Heaven, thank you for providing our family with food again.

We will eat gratefully.

I want to work. Studying doesn't suit me.

Hmm, Vincent. You know Goupil's Gallery, right?

Yes, the one that Uncle Cent operates...

Yes. I'll talk to him. If all goes well, maybe you'll be able to work at the branch in The Hague.

Okay.

Vincent's going to The Hague?

That night, Vincent could not sleep well. He knew he wanted to make money as soon as possible to help his family's financial situation. However, when he thought about being apart from his family, he became very sad.

Theo, I know you're not asleep.

Vincent, don't leave! Stay with us!

I'll earn a lot of money and come back. Then, I'll be able to buy you everything you've ever wanted to eat.

But...

Voila! Theo, stop crying and take a look at this.

I drew a picture of the wheat field that we used to play in together.

I can't see it well because it's dark in here.

Well, this is you. This is me. Can you see it?

Theo, I'm going to miss you, too, but let's just try to be patient. Whenever you miss me, look at this picture.

Can you promise me that? I'll make sure to write to you.

Vincent left his hometown and went to The Hague where the Goupil Gallery was located.

So, you must be the Vincent who's supposed to work here starting today.

Yes, manager.

You're going to have to describe the works of art to the people who come to the gallery. Do you know anything about artwork?

Well, I like to draw... But I don't know much yet.

22

Then it'll probably be better for you to sell posters and photographs. If you have spare time while working, study the artwork.

Study the artwork?

Yes. We need to know how the motifs of each piece are expressed in these works of art.

That way we can talk to the clients and sell these works of art to them.

Yes, I understand.

Vincent worked at the Goupil Gallery in The Hague selling photographs and posters of paintings. Sincere Vincent won the hearts of many people.

When interacting with people, Vincent was very lively. However, when he was alone, he kept thinking about his family.

When Vincent returned to the boarding house that he was staying at he started to write a letter to his younger brother, Theo.

26

Dear Theo,
How are you doing? I'm adapting well to life here. I like working at the gallery, too.

I haven't sold many paintings yet, but I'm happy that I get to interact with the people and talk to them about the paintings. I miss you, Theo, and the rest of the family, too.

Vincent started writing letters to Theo, who he got along with better than anyone else.

In his letter, he wrote about life, the paintings, minor things, etc. Theo received the letter and replied. Ever since then, Vincent and Theo continued to write each other letters and had a very strong brotherhood.

02 Kicked out of the Gallery

After working at the Goupil branch in The Hague for 4 years, Vincent's abilities were recognized and he ended up moving to the branch in London, England.

Could you put the luggage over here?

29

I'm late with my introduction. I'm Eugenie Loyer. I'm the daughter of the landlady of this place.

The first time that Vincent saw Eugenie, he fell for her at first glance.

E-Eugenie Loyer...

If you need anything, please let me know.

Eugenie! She's an angel!

Everything looked beautiful to Vincent because he had fallen in love. Thanks to Eugenie, the unfamiliar and strange city of London became a warm and friendly place.

The paintings on this side cost 1 pound each.

The ones over here cost 5 pounds each.

I guess this guy must be having a good day?

Maybe. I guess he likes it here in London.

Vincent continued to fall deeper in love with Eugenie. Then one day, Vincent and Eugenie were walking back from church together.

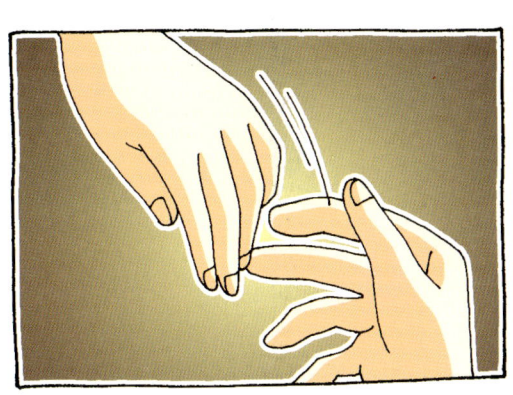

Why... what's wrong?

Vincent, I'm going to pretend I did not just hear that.

I already have a fiance.

Wh-what? A fiance?

I don't love you.

I'm sorry, Vincent.

Eugenie!

33

Vincent's confession to his first love ended badly. He was very hurt and scarred as a result.

Eugenie, why...

Vincent lost all motivation. He did not feel like masking his sadness by smiling and being kind in front of the customers in order to sell paintings.

Excuse me, I'm interested in buying this painting. Could you tell me how much it costs?

This one costs 1 pound. That one costs 5 pounds.

No, I wasn't asking about these posters. I'm talking about the paintings. I want the actual paintings.

That's not what I'm responsible for. Go ask someone else!

Wh-what's wrong with me? How could I yell at a customer?

I-I'm so sorry. What were you saying before?

36

After having his heart broken and getting kicked out of London, Vincent moved to Paris and resorted to religion to appease his heartache.

Vincent, it seems like you read the Bible whenever you have any free time.

When I read the Bible, I feel calmer.

Why don't you go take a look at paintings instead? If you see any good ones, bring them to the gallery, too.

Paintings?

There's a hall that's exhibiting Millet's* work posthumously. There has been a lot of interest in this painter recently. This is a good opportunity for you to develop a new eye for looking at art.

Millet...

A little while after Vincent started working in Paris, Millet passed away and there was a posthumous exhibition of Millet's artwork.

In order to find paintings that were good enough to be sold at the gallery, Vincent went to the Millet exhibition.

*Millet: A French Painter. He liked to focus on the landscapes and lifestyles of peasants. His masterpieces were the *Curfew Bell*, *Gleaning* and so on.

Millet was a Realist painter.

Traditional Realist painters do not paint about things like myths that we can't see or about something from the Bible. They get inspired by everyday life and paint about it.

Millet was representative of these Realist painters.

Vincent was shocked after having seen Millet's paintings. Finding the source of a painting's subject matter from everyday life was, at the moment, completely against the flow of art and was something new.

I can feel the emotions of the people shown in these paintings. I can't believe this one painting could touch and shake a person's heart so much. Isn't something like this what a real painting is?

If I can I want to create paintings like this, too.

After seeing Millet's work, Vincent came to adore the work of Realist painters. At the gallery, there were often disputes between Vincent and those who would not acknowledge Realism.

You there. I'm looking for a painting to buy and put in my house. Do you have any recommendations?

Sir, how about this one?

Excuse me? How dare you!

Sir, what's wrong? What's going on here?

This is the first time something like this has happened to me! How dare this jerk who doesn't know anything about art treat me this way!

Sorry. We'll call over a different employee for you.

Vincent, come see me in my office. Right this instant!

43

Vincent was starting to become a more and more troublesome and cranky employee. The Vincent who used to talk a lot with customers as well as the other employees at the gallery became a loner. He decided to secretly leave for vacation.

No one understood how Vincent was feeling. Eventually, because of his poor work attitude, Vincent was fired from the gallery.

03 • A Pastor's Path

CD1 Track 19 ▶

After losing his job, Vincent returned to his hometown in the Netherlands. Vincent would look for a new job while also relaxing.

Vincent, could you repeat that?

I want to become a pastor like you, Father.

Why all of a sudden? Becoming a pastor is not as easy as you probably think it is.

I think that all the things that have happened to me recently were trials that the Heavens wanted me to face. After going through all of that, I started thinking about becoming a pastor.

You know about the qualifications that one needs in order to become a pastor, right? You need to attend college.

Yes, I know.

I don't know if you'll be able to put up with all those years.

I can do it. I'm very desperate right now.

Alright, I'm feeling better now that you've found your path. Let's arrange for you to stay with Uncle Jan in Amsterdam as you prepare for your studies.

Vincent listened to his father's words and went to Amsterdam.

Vincent, if anything is bothering you or if anything is wrong while you're studying, feel free to talk to me about it. I will help you as much as I can.

Yes, thank you very much.

Greek and Latin were requirements for the exam to become a pastor. Thanks to the help of his relatives, Vincent was able to be tutored by the famous Costa.

Vincent, how long has it been since I've been tutoring you?

It's been a little under half a year.

Then, that's a problem. Your Latin is coming along fine, but you've shown no improvement in your Greek.

I'm sorry, teacher.

No, there's no reason for you to apologize to me. However, at this rate, you won't be able to pass the qualifications exam. Please try a little bit harder.

Yes, teacher.

Vincent's tutor, Costa, poured his heart into teaching Vincent. Vincent studied very hard. However, even after one year passed, Vincent's skills had not grown much.

I have something to tell you.

What?

*missionary: A person who guides non-Christians to have faith.

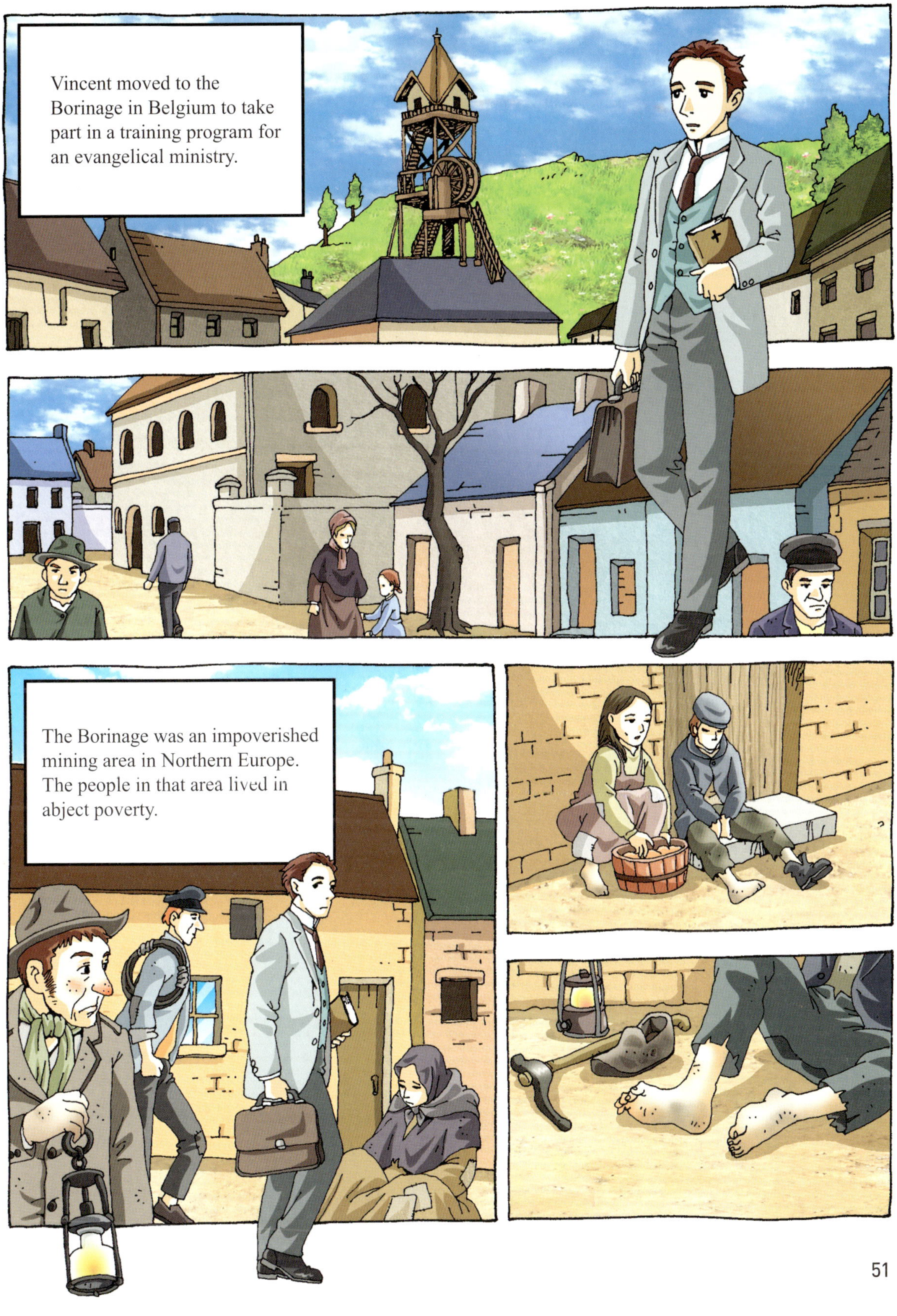

Vincent moved to the Borinage in Belgium to take part in a training program for an evangelical ministry.

The Borinage was an impoverished mining area in Northern Europe. The people in that area lived in abject poverty.

The next day, Vincent set out to look for the miners so that he could spread the words of the Bible to them.

The miners' lives were miserable. It was devastating for Vincent to see these miners who struggled to live every single day.

Work after taking a lunch break.

You're a missionary, correct?

Yes.

Haha,
I'll be fine.

O-okay,
then...

The people of The Bornage had nothing to eat and nothing to wear. In addition, whenever a coal mine collapsed, many people would lose their lives.

Whenever Vincent finished work and returned home, he would start drawing the people of The Bornage and send the drawings to Theo. This was because Vincent wanted to show Theo how meaningful spreading God's words could be in such a miserable place.

Vincent shared everything that he had with the poor. He thought of it as practicing the Bible message that says to love thy neighbors.

I'm looking for the missionary, Vincent van Gogh, who is part of the training program. Do you know where I can find him?

What for?

A-are you Vincent van Gogh?

56

Yes, but...

I'm the supervisor who supervises the missionaries! Anyway, what is with your outfit? If you go around wearing such clothes, people would laugh at the church. You look like a homeless person.

What's wrong with my outfit? I gave away and shared everything that I had with the people here because I wanted to be one with them.

The church is supposed to give people hope. It needs to be as beautiful as the Heavens, and the people who work there have to be lively and clean!

Have you seen the people who live around here? What's the point of being completely different from the people here, and being a beautiful and clean church by itself?

Look, Vincent. I don't feel like arguing with you. Clearly, a missionary like you is just tainting and disgracing the church. You're fired.

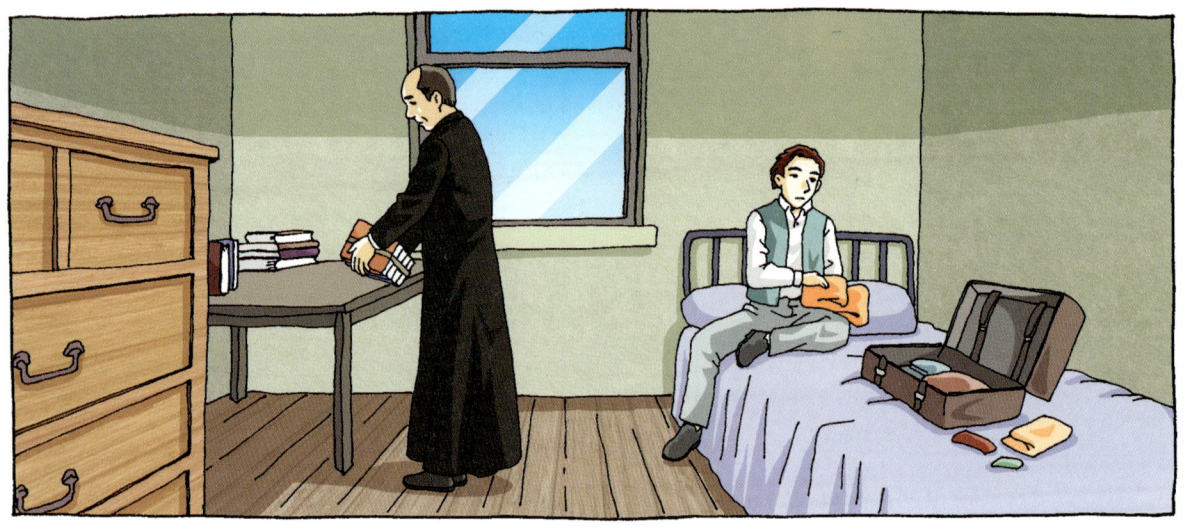

Did I really do something wrong, Pastor? I was just practicing God's words.

I'm sorry. There isn't much I can say, but no matter what kind of work you do do not lose or forget about your ability to love and care for the poor.

Ha. Pastor, everything that I have done up until now has failed. Do you think I'll be able to start over with a new job again?

Stay strong, Vincent.

Everyone has a path that has been destined to them from the Heavens. You just haven't found your path yet, that's all.

Sniff, sniff. Pastor! I really want to be able to help the people here. It wasn't enough to just simply spread the word of God.

I wanted to go deep into their lives and share with them! I guess I'm not even allowed to do such a small job. I'm just an idiot who can't seem to do anything right!

I understand how you must feel. However, even I...

Wait, did you draw this picture?

Huh?

Oh, that's just something I drew in my spare time.

It's a really great piece of work. You can really feel the worries and hardships that these people are feeling in the picture. Whoever sees this picture would want to help out the people of the Bornage.

Vincent. Your drawings have an authenticity and genuineness about them. How about you try being an artist?

Drawing?

Vincent recalled the emotions he had felt when he saw Millet's work for the first time ever. The painting of the simple and true lives of the poor had broken his heart more than any painting of a myth or Bible scene could.

Would I be able to do it, too? Drawing the simple and sincere lifestyles of regular people instead of drawing the heroes from myths and the miracles from the Bible!

04 •Painting

CD1 Track 27 ▶

After deciding to focus on art, Vincent did not let himself waste any time. Vincent went to the Netherlands in order to see his relative, Anton Mauve, who was a painter.

TAP TAP TAP

Vincent! What brings you here?

Anton, may I come in?

Of course, welcome.

I heard you were training to be a missionary but that plan failed. What are you doing now?

Actually, that's why I'm here. I want to be a painter.

A painter?

Yes. Do you remember how I used to work at Goupil's Gallery when I was younger? During that time, I had the opportunity to look at a lot of different paintings, and I fell in love with paintings. It took me until now to realize that.

A love for paintings? It's hard to become a painter based solely on that.

That's why I came here to find you. I never properly learned how to draw pictures.

At the time, Theo was working at an art gallery selling paintings just as Vincent had done when he was younger. Vincent did not have enough money to pay for a place to stay, so he borrowed money from Theo in order to do so.

I'm looking for a place to stay.

Come, follow me. I have a place that's perfect for one person to live in.

Vincent, your drawings are truthful.

Huh?

With a little help and polishing, you could draw some very good pictures.

*still life: A painting or drawing of an arrangement of objects such as flowers or fruit.

Vincent worked hard and practiced drawing a lot. He built up hours of practice and developed his skills. Then one day...

Hahahaha. Anton, Anton!

What is it?

I received a request for a drawing! I'm going to get paid if I draw 12 pictures of landscapes for the customer. Hahaha!

Really?

Now I'm a painter who can sell his artwork!

Vincent, don't mistake yourself.

Huh?

The person requested pictures from you simply out of courtesy. You're not that good yet. No one is interested in your work.

How could he say such things? He could've just been happy for me and congratulated me.

After hearing such cold remarks from Mauve, Vincent did not have good feelings towards him.

Vincent, your work is too dark.

I made it dark on purpose. I'm trying to express the fact that there is no light. I'm trying to show that the owner of these shoes has lived a turbulent life.

Haha, what you're saying is plausible, but paintings like this won't sell. Start all over.

Give me your paintbrush.

I'll figure it out on my own.

Especially this part, right here, doesn't match with the rest of the painting because it's been painted on so thickly.

I told you I painted this all dark in order to express the shoe owner's turbulent life! Stop interfering when you don't even know!

V-Vincent?

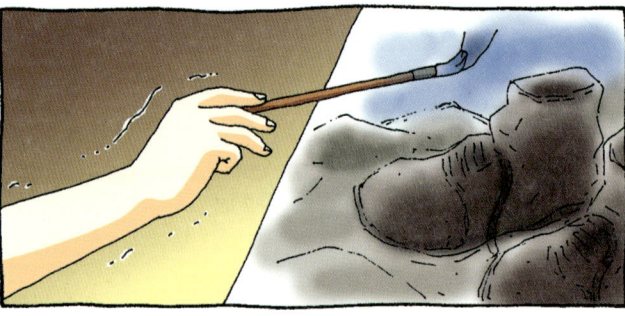

Vincent did not want to have any more conflicts with Mauve, so he decided to go back to his hometown. In order to pay for his unpaid rent, Vincent wrote a letter to Theo.

Dear Theo,

Do you think you could send me some money? I'm really late on paying my rent. In order to pay you back for all the money that I borrowed, I'll send you my paintings so that you could sell them. I'm going to go back to our hometown. I'm going to draw whatever I want when I'm there.

Back in his hometown, Vincent would get up very early in the morning and leave to work on his drawings. He would not come home until very late at night because he was embarassed at the fact that he was almost 30 years old. He felt like he was too old to still be such a burden on his family.

Where on earth are you going again, Vincent?

Sigh.

Because Vincent had failed at everything he had ever done, and because he returned to his hometown broke, there wasn't a place that would welcome him. Vincent would go around looking for poor people who were living hard lives, and he would spend time with them.

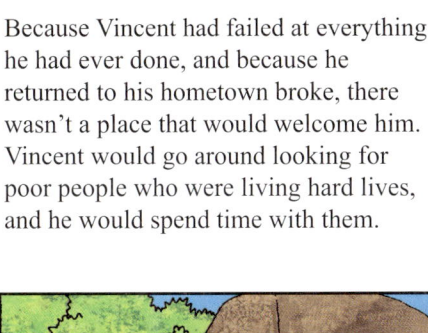

Welcome, Vincent.

Were you in the middle of eating?

Yup, I was eating a potato. Would you like one, too?

No, it's okay. Don't worry about me and eat up.

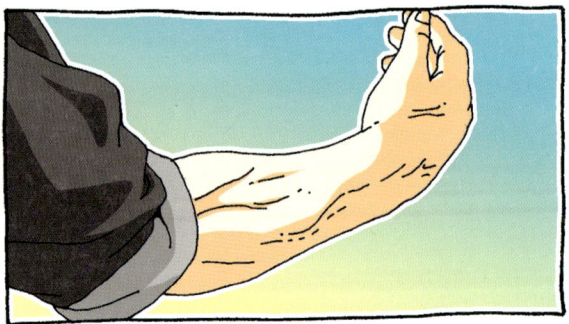

Look at those rough hands. He probably worked incredibly hard all day just so he could eat a few potatoes. He's just grateful that he doesn't have to starve.

His family cares about each other so much that everyone's trying to share whatever it is that they have. They look so happy! This is it. This is exactly the kind of thing that I wanted to draw.

Vincent wanted to capture the preciousness of everyday life in his artwork just as Millet had done. He drew a picture of the poor farmer's family as they were eating. This painting, *The Potato Eaters*, was a significant and special piece of work for Vincent because it was this piece that led him one step closer to his artistic goals.

Vincent sent *The Potato Eaters* to his brother, Theo, who was working at the gallery. Vincent was positive that this painting, that he had worked so hard on, would sell for a lot of money.

Theo, that painting is too grayish. On top of that, it's a painting of farmers so the aristocrats wouldn't even be interested in it.

But, Millet drew farmers, too. I think you can really see that the painter's sincerity has been poured into this painting.

What nonsense! At least in Millet's paintings, the farmers looked like people. These people look like weirdos. Look at their postures. Look how bent over they are. They look more like apes than people.

B-but, this...

Get rid of this right away. If you like it so much, then you keep it.

Sorry, bro.

Meanwhile, Vincent sent a lithograph of *The Potato Eaters* to his painter friend, Rappard.

Vincent, there's a letter for you. Rappard?

Oh, it's from my friend.

Is it a positive letter?

Haha, we'll see.

Psh, he obviously doesn't know how to look at real art! I will never look at or care about you ever again!

Rappard's evaluation of *The Potato Eaters* was negative. Vincent was so angry that he vented all his emotions in a letter that he was writing to Theo.

Dear Theo,

Rappard says that The Potato Eaters looks like something I rushed to paint and was unprepared for. He doesn't even know how many sketches I made before I actually painted this. He doesn't know a thing and he's acting like he's so high and mighty and dismissing my work...

78

What angers me the most is that he said the figures in the painting have unproportionate bodies and that the painting was junk. He says that the people's hands are too big and that their postures are awkward. This is ridiculous. I purposely exaggerated their hands to express that these laborers use their hands to survive.

The hands may be large and rough but it's because of those hands that the whole family can live in harmony and not starve to death. If people are going to complain about body proportions then they might as well go look at photographs of people instead of paintings!

Stupid jerk! He doesn't even know the significance of the hands and he has the guts to carelessly criticize my work!

05 In France

Vincent decided not to worry about what other people thought about his work. However, all the negative criticism and feedback hurt Vincent.

In order to study more about painting, Vincent went to the Academy of Antwerp. He enrolled in the Academy of Fine Art in Antwerp and started studying.

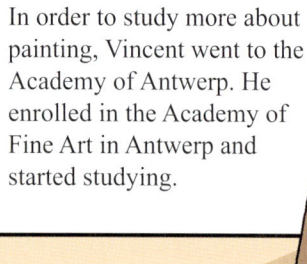

Pictures aren't photographs. Drawing things exactly the way they are is pointless.

What? You're unbelievably outrageous. Get some skills before you say such things!

The Art class at the Academy did not work for Vincent. At the time, art was praised for being highly elaborate and exact. However, Vincent considered those kinds of drawings and paintings as dead.

What idiots! An exact drawing of the statue doesn't make that drawing a real drawing. There has to be some life coming through from the picture!

Wait, what! What's this?

There's life and color in this painting, and the technique used to emphasize what needs to be expressed is simple and bold. This has a livelihood that you can't find at the Academy of Fine Art!

Welcome.

Where did those paintings outside come from? They're so beautiful that I'm almost speechless!

Oh, you must be talking about the Japanese paintings. *Ukiyo-e* is the name of the technique used in those paintings.

Ukiyo-e? Is this a painting of Japanese nobility?

That's not nobility, but a playactor. The Japanese *Ukiyo-e* genre captures the images of common people.

Is there a place I could go to see more paintings like this?

If you go out, make a left and keep going straight, you'll see a an art museum. Paintings and ceramics from China and Japan are on exhibition there.

Thank you.

After seeing the *Ukiyo-e* paintings, Vincent was reassured that his way of thinking and drawing was not incorrect. With that thought in his head, he no longer felt to need to stay and study art in this strange and unfamiliar city.

Vincent left Antwerp and went to Paris where Theo was working.

Bro, is that really you?

Theo!

Theo, it's been so long! I missed you so much!

When did you get to Paris? Why didn't you call me and let me know ahead of time?

Don't you think it's more exciting to see me since I came so randomly?

It's *Sunrise* by Monet and it's an Impressionist masterpiece.

Impressionist?

Yup. These painters believe that making paintings of landscapes and figures that are exact like photographs is pointless.

Really?

Look at this piece. There are no clear lines or shapes. Impressionist painters don't draw things exactly the way they are, but instead, they highlight the change and beauty of the colors.

Theo, could you introduce me to the person who painted this? I want to meet him.

Sure.

I feel great that we have a new friend here today!

Vincent, is it true that you're Theo's older brother?

Yes, it's true. I saw all of your paintings and I wanted to meet you guys so I kept bugging Theo to help make it happen.

Haha, all of us are poor painters. We paint pictures that just won't sell. You'll soon come to regret having hung out with us.

It's my pleasure. I was getting bored of the Art at the Academy.

For example, I use Pointillism. Nature uses light to show its colors, but I believe that that light is made up of a lot of little dots. Thus, I express that thought with my art.

Don't stress about it, Vincent. He makes it sound complicated but really he just draws pictures by drawing a bunch of little dots.

Gauguin, you boring Secession* jerk!

I don't know what all these terms and different forms of art techniques are. I just hate the kind of art that they were doing at the Academy. That's all I know.

Then, Vincent you can be a Secession artist, too. Join me! We can be on the same boat, haha!

Huh?

Vincent had an attentive and quiet personality, unlike Gauguin who had a cheerful and haughty personality. Vincent liked Gauguin because he was outgoing. Vincent and Gauguin started becoming close friends.

*Secession: Artists who separated from traditional academic art in pursuit of free expression for artists.

So, "Secession" is the term describing the break away from academic art. Pointillism is when you dismantle the light and make pictures out of a lot of little dots...

The painters stayed up having a late-night debate. However, Vincent felt that all these rules and techniques were locking the pictures up behind their frames. This withered his excitement about having met these painters.

Hey, bro! You're back? Did you have a lot of fun today, too?

Why do you seem so tired and down?

Sigh. Theo, I don't think I should hang out with them that much anymore.

Why?

I don't like art theory and stuff like that. I just want to draw whatever I feel like drawing.

Yeah, that's what's best for a painter. Keep your chin up, bro.

You're the only one who really understands and supports me.

Vincent just stayed in his room and started to draw. He focused on doing a self-portrait. However, not only did he want to capture his outer appearance, but he also wanted to show the changes inside of him by using free brush strokes that were independent from any techniques or rules.

Vincent lived in Paris for two years. During those two years, Vincent drew over 200 paintings. To say that he kept drawing with out ever resting would not even be an exaggeration.

How are your paintings going, bro?

Look. This is what I've been doing for the last week.

The motifs in Vincent's paintings were changing from the theme of daily lives of common people to that of beautiful nature and natural light. However, Paris failed to satisfy this changing Vincent's needs.

Sigh, this isn't it...

What I want to draw isn't a town like this. Isn't there a place around here where the warm sun beats down on nature and draws out its natural light and colors?

I need to find another place... like a nice little village.

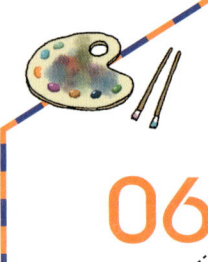

06 Under the Arles Sun

CD2 Track 10 ▶

Are you okay, Vincent?

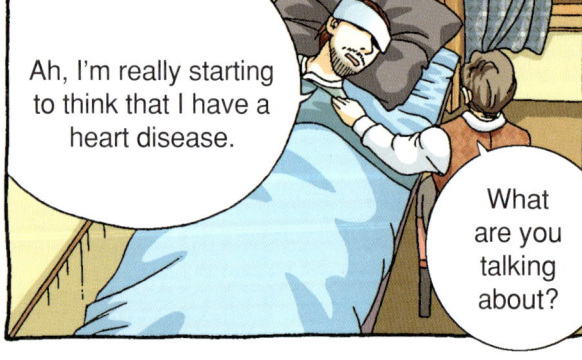

Ah, I'm really starting to think that I have a heart disease.

What are you talking about?

Theo, I want to draw the fresh air and the bright sun. I want to draw the grass dancing as the wind blows through it. I want to draw the glaring sun that makes people squint their eyes.

But there are no warm, scenic places like that in this town. I want to see nature. I want to capture the primary colors that the sky and land create together on canvas.

Oh my gosh. You're saying that that's why you're sick?

Theo, I think I'm going to have to move down South to Arles. In Arles, it's still warm in the winter so I'll always be able to draw the things I want to draw.

You think so too, right? I should leave right way, Theo!

Bro... You really were sick because of your art, huh?

Arles? Yeah, that place would have all the scenic views that you've been wanting to draw.

Vincent left to go to Arles, which was located in Southern France. As soon as he left town, he felt like the sickness he had inside of him was all gone and better.

Arles was a beautiful place. It was just as warm, sunny and green as Vincent had always imagined. Vincent dug his easel into the ground so that he could draw whenever and however long he wanted to.

Vincent tirelessly drew from day to night. He was constantly drawing and working so hard that the village people thought that he wasn't sane.

When the day came to an end, Vincent would go to a 24 hour café. He would sit there and sketch while he enjoyed the night. Vincent was a regular at the Night Café that he always went to.

Vincent, do you like this place?

The Night Café was open 24 hours a day, which allowed people who didn't have money to sleep in a hotel to come in and wait out the night. Vincent loved that about this café because it was helpful to the poor. Thus, his picture of the café was lively and portrayed the lights that were always on and the people who moved about inside every night.

Yes. No matter what part of Arles I draw, it always looks good.

Oh wow. Even our café looks better in your painting!

Winters in Arles were warm. Vincent would be in his house, drawing pictures nonstop of the scenery and of sunflowers.

Vincent started to think that it was a waste that he was the only one who got to see how beautiful Arles was. Thus, he decided to invite his friends to Arles, since it was surrounded with beautiful scenery that they could draw pictures of.

Painters' Village...

Theo, could you do me a favor and invite my friends from Paris over to Arles? I want to make this a place where painters could come and draw and help each other improve their work.

Did you say Arles?

Yes, Mr. Seurat. My brother thought it'd be nice if Impressionist painters could go there and work on their art while helping each other improve as well.

But we don't have to go all the way to the village to do that. I don't want to go.

Well... I'm more comfortable working from home.

Sorry, Theo. I would love to go but I don't have the money.

Arles?

Yes. If you need help with the expenses, I'd be willing to help you.

Painters' Village... That sounds pretty cool.

Does this mean you'll go, Mr. Gauguin?

But Theo, why didn't Vincent invite me himself?

Oh, well...

I think Vincent sees you as a mother figure.

That's not it. He's so busy drawing pictures and painting that he's a bit frazzled so he asked me to invite you guys as a favor. If you go to Arles and see what my brother has been working on, you'd probably be very surprised.

Hahaha, I'm jealous of Vincent for having such a wonderful brother like you. I will go down to Arles as soon as I'm done dealing with a few things here.

Dear Vincent,

I contacted some of the painters that you were really close with but not that many people said they could attend. Don't be disappointed though. Gauguin said that he would go to see you in Arles. I'll keep trying to persuade the others as well.

Vincent, you seem to be in a good mood today. Did something happen?

Yes. My friend from France has decided to come visit me here. My friend is a better painter than I am so there's going to be a lot to learn.

After receiving Theo's letter, Vincent was extremely excited. He began to clean and decorate his house in preparation for his good friend who he hadn't seen in a while.

Oh wow, that's wonderful. Come inside for a second. I want to give you some freshly baked bread as a congratulatory gift.

Thank you, but I'll have to pass. I have to hurry because I have a lot to do.

In October, 1888, Gauguin arrived at Arles.

Thanks for coming, Gauguin. I wish everyone else would hurry and come here, too.

Hmm, I don't know. I don't think many painters would want to come to a village like this.

What?

Either way, it's good to see you, Vincent. It's been a whole year since I last saw you. Do you like this place that much?

Yeah. Paris can't measure up to how awesome Arles is. You'll see what I mean soon enough.

It's a whole sunflower.

Do you like it? It's a present for you. The yellow sunflower symbolizes hope. It hopes and wishes for our dreams to come true. I plan on focusing on drawing sunflowers for the time being.

The sunflower looks like the blazing sun. I can feel your intense passion from it.

And so, Vincent and Gauguin started living together. The two of them had much respect for each other.

Yes. I worked on this while I waited for you to come to Arles.

Is this your self-portrait?

Haha, thanks. I really like it. But why'd you draw the head shaved?

I guess I was waiting for you piously like the monks who shave their heads. I put my respect for you into the painting.

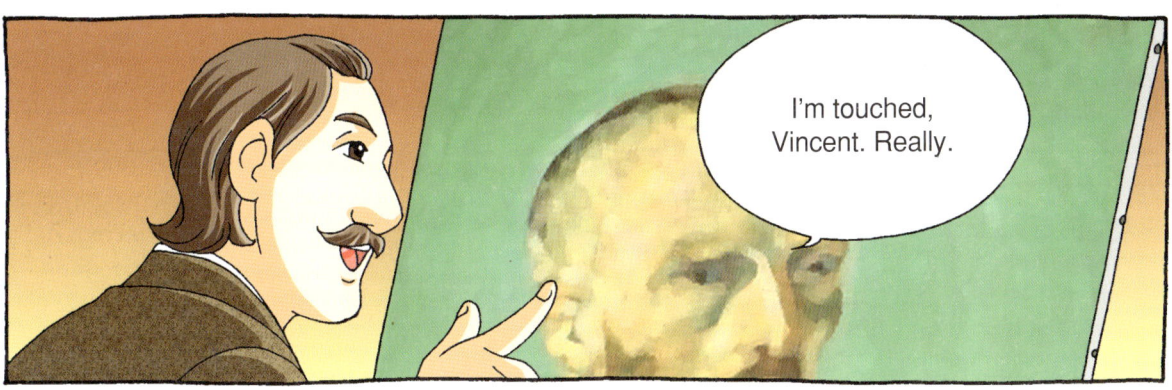

I'm touched, Vincent. Really.

Vincent and Gauguin would talk to each other about their paintings' motifs, and they would happily paint in each others company. But before long, the two men started having problems.

Vincent, aren't you tired f drawing sunflowers?

I told you. The sunflower looks like the blazing sun and it represents our hope for a bright future.

So you think that the sun will shower us with blessings? Don't you think that's a childish idea? I think you've drawn enough sunflowers. You don't need to do this anymore.

I draw what I want to draw. You don't get to tell me what to draw and what not to draw.

You should be thankful for the advice. When I look at you these days, I feel like you're working so hard on such pointless drawings.

Pointless drawings? Enough is enough. Stop it before I get even angrier!

Argh! I can't seem to get through to you!

Gauguin! This kind of behavior is unforgivable!

SLAM

Jerk!

Vincent and Gauguin had different perspectives when looking at art. They also had different personalities, hobbies, etc. Vincent was a very emotional and sensitive guy so he was really hurt by a lot of the things that Gauguin had said to him.

Phew, I'm getting tired of life here. Arles is really just a poor village.

Stop it. I like this place.

The relationship between the two of them got worse every day. Then one day...

That's a new picture. Who are you painting?

You.

M-me?

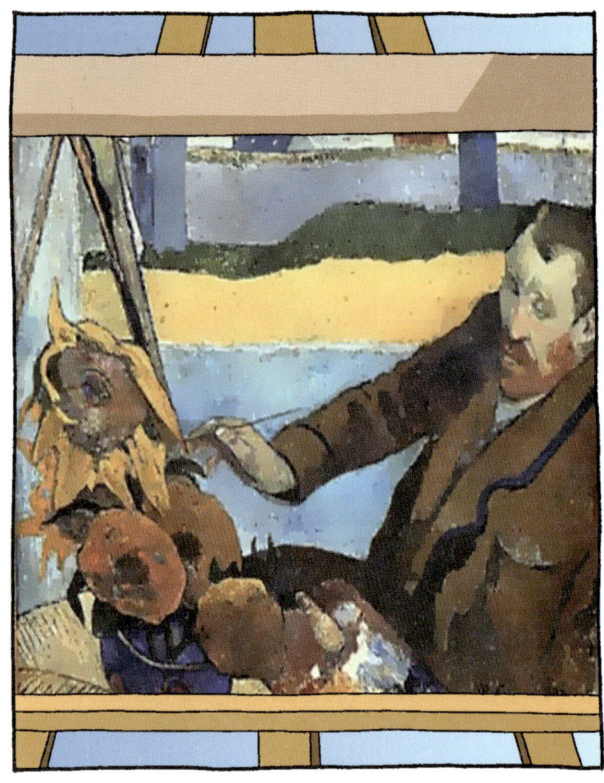

Wait a second. You're saying that this is me? Are you trying to say that you see me as a lunatic?

What are you talking about? I was just impressed by you struggling so hard to fix the sunflower. I was just expressing my respect for that.

Vincent did not like the painting that Gauguin drew of him. This was because, in the painting, Vincent's eyes were barely showing, but the sunflower looked like a big eye that was watching him.

Why is the paintbrush so skinny? Where is the canvas?

Vincent laughed with a ridiculous look on his face. He figured that the skinny brush and almost non-existant canvas was supposed to mean that he was lousy at painting.

Do you not see it? It's very skinny but you are definitely holding a paintbrush in this painting. Also, the canvas is laying at an angle so you can't really see it.

Haha, really?

Vincent came to the conclusion that Gauguin was mocking him through his paintings.

What's wrong? Is there a problem?

No, thank you for drawing such a wonderful picture.

From then on, the two men would fight every day. Even though there were a lot of problems they had to face in everyday life, they particularly fought about their artwork a lot. This was because neither of the two wanted to be the bigger man and yield.

What? She operates a bar, so I drew her to look like a bar owner. What's wrong with that?

What is this? How dare you draw the Night Café's owner like this?

This lady has helped me a lot and I am very grateful to her. The lady in this picture looks like a vulgar and gross woman!

No, my picture is realistic. You just unnecessarily held her in vain. Does that make any sense? Whenever you draw her you make her look so lady like but she works at a bar!

How dare you mock the people I care about! I can put up with you insulting me but this is unforgivable!

Vincent, pictures come from inside the painters' hearts. I was just being faithful to my heart.

How could you ignore the fact that this lady is someone that's really important to your friend? You complete jerk!

Haha, you're really funny! This is why your paintings never sell! I heard you never ever sold a single one of your paintings! At least there are people out there who actually want my paintings and come look for me!

Wh-what?

115

07 The Last Artistic Soul

Vincent was unconscious for a very long time. When he finally regained consciousness Gauguin and Theo were watching over him in the hospital.

Mmm....

T-Theo...

Try to relax, bro. Your condition needs to stabilize.

So you were watching over me. I love you, Theo.

Vincent, you need to calm down and rest so that you can heal faster.

I'm okay now. This isn't going to affect my drawing or painting so let's go back home.

Vincent was released from the hospital with bandages wrapped around his head. The villagers who saw Vincent treated him like a psychopath and distanced themselves from him.

Don't stare at him. He's a dangerous person.

WAAAAHHH

Hey, don't cry. I'm not a scary person.

Go away. Don't come any closer! Somebody, help!

118

119

Stop it! Everyone! My brother's not going to hurt anybody!

Hurry. Let's go back home, bro.

The villagers are uncomfortable about living in the same village as you. I think we're going to have to leave this town as soon as possible.

Vincent followed Theo's suggestion and left Arles to go to the asylum in Saint-Rémy.

Don't ever come back! You crazy fool!

At the asylum in Saint-Rémy, Vincent spent every day drawing as always. If he didn't draw, he didn't feel alive.

Vincent created many works of art at the asylum. One of such works was *Starry Night*, a painting, in which he drew the stars as huge swirls. This would become Vincent's masterpiece and receive a lot of love.

Dear Theo,

I don't know anyone in this whole hospital and this place is pretty deserted. The only thing that makes me feel the least bit alive is drawing. The sky always greets me though. It's not a dark and black sky, but instead it's the blue night sky that moves towards me. When the wind runs around and the clouds dance, the stars sparkle and shine as they give off a warm light.

Whenever Vincent had a seizure, he would show some serious symptoms such as eating paint, etc. Other than that, however, Vincent lived a pretty peaceful life.

One day after staying at the asylum in Saint-Rémy for over one year...

Mr. van Gogh, a package has arrived for you from your brother.

Mercure... de France....

Hey bro, I put some of your works on exhibit along with some works by other Impressionist painters, and now there's an article about your work in this magazine. It was written by the critic, Albert Aurier. Be sure to read it.

Vincent van Gogh lives with nature and his palette creates joy...

H-he is a great artist!

With faith and love, he had a dream of creating a place of Utopia on earth...

HA HA HA!

125

This is just the beginning! Woo!

Soon after, Vincent received some more good news.

There's a letter for you from your brother, Mr. van Gogh.

What's this? It's a check for 400 francs.

Vincent! After your review in the magazine, your works are attracting a lot of attention. Your work The Red Vineyard sold for 400 francs so I sent you the money.

127

I did it! I, Vincent van Gogh, did it! Hahahaha!

March, 1890.
In France, an exhibition called the "Salon des Independants" opened up. This was an exhibit for the young artists who were up and coming and causing a new wind to blow in the art world. At this exhibit, ten of Vincent van Gogh's works were exhibited.

Hmm.

Aren't you Dr. Gachet? Do you like this painting? My brother drew it.

It's been a while since I've seen you, Theo. This painting makes me feel like the sky is alive and moving. I really love this painting.

Haha, my brother would've been extremely happy to hear that.

Where's your brother? He didn't come to the exhibition?

Unfortunately, he's sick so he's at the hospital.

Oh, actually, now that I think about it, you would probably be able to help.

Is it a mental illness?

Yes, but as long as can draw, there are no major problems except the occasional seizure.

Okay, then send your brother to Auvers, where I live. I'll take care of him.

Really? Thank you, Dr. Gachet.

Vincent went to Auvers to stay with Dr. Gachet. He would draw pictures all day and night as if his life depended on it.

Vincent, could you draw a portrait of me?

I really enjoy your artwork. If you could draw a portrait of me, I would be so very happy.

Thank you. I didn't have a model to draw so it was hard. Now I get tired of even drawing self-portraits.

129

Vincent carefully drew a picture of Dr. Gachet who had been taking good care of him. Vincent wanted to capture his gratitude for Dr. Gachet within the portrait. A few days later, Dr. Gachet was able to see the finished portrait.

Surprising. Yeah, this is my true self.

Vincent, you saw right through me. You saw that deep inside, I was tired and exhausted.

I'm glad and relieved to know that you like the portrait.

Hahaha. You seem to be able to look inside a person's mind better than me and I'm a psychiatrist. I've never met another painter quite like you.

Because there was someone there who loved his paintings, Vincent was able to draw more happily. Every morning, as soon as he woke up, Vincent would begin drawing. Sometimes there were days when he would finish multiple works of art.

However, Vincent's paintings didn't sell. It hadn't taken long before his life went back to the way it used to be.

Theo, I need to borrow money from you again. I have no dignity left.

Vincent, is something wrong these days?

I haven't gotten a reply from Theo. This has never happened before...

Theo?

Theo's probably in the Netherlands. He said he was going to visit his hometown with his family. He probably didn't get to see your letter yet, either.

Wh-what?

After finding out that Theo had left for their hometown without even contacting him, Vincent began to worry.

I can't believe I'm so anxiety-ridden just because I found Theo isn't around here. I must be some idiot who can't function or live without having his younger brother around.

Now there aren't even any people who want to purchase my paintings. At least back then when I couldn't sell any paintings, I still had hope for the future...

Now, I don't have any hope.

Vincent, you're an idiot!

How long are you going to burden Theo for? How much longer do you plan on scrubbing off of your younger brother?

You don't deserve to live! You're just making life harder for everyone else!

SLAM SLAM

I'm sorry, Theo. Please forgive your horrible, older brother.

Vincent spent time sitting around helplessly, not doing anything at all. Even when Dr. Gachet tried to console Vincent, he could not cheer him up.

Ha, now... I can't do anything... except...

Whenever Vincent thought about how he couldn't succeed no matter how hard he struggled to be a painter, he would also think about how sorry he felt toward his brother, Theo. Thinking about it heavily crushed Vincent's heart. Vincent resented the god who had given him such a cruel fate.

And in order to prevent the god from causing more pain in his life, Vincent decided to put an end to his own destiny. One day when the sky sank as heavily as Vincent's heart had...

POW

Vincent went out onto the most beautiful, golden wheatfield in Auvers.

My dear brother Theo,

I know I always tell you this but you were never just simply an art dealer. You were my companion and together we made art. Throughout my entire life, no one loved me or supported me as much as you did.

I place my fate in the hands of my artwork. Now I feel like that half has been achieved. The other half has yet to be fulfilled, but may never need to be in my lifetime. Someday my paintings will tell the whole story. However, as of right now, there is nothing I could do.

Vincent tried to commit suicide using a pistol, but he didn't die until two days later on July 29, 1890. Vincent's funeral service was sorrowful.

I should've taken care of my brother better... I became negligent because he was in the care of a doctor. I'm so sorry. I'm so sorry, Vincent.

Theo felt sick with guilt because he felt that he had neglected his brother who had been reliant on him. Theo became so depressed that he developed psychosis.

Bro, why are you inside the picture? Come out, now!

Honey! What's wrong with you? Please calm down.

Sob. My brother isn't dead! He's right there!

Theo ended up passing away six months after the day of his older brother's death. In 1914, Theo's grave was moved beside Vincent's so that the two brothers could be together forever.

There was one other person who had loved Vincent's art just as much as Theo had. This person was Theo's wife, Jo.

Hello, are you looking for someone?

I... am trying to make a book.

What kind of book? A novel? Or a poem book?

Letters that my husband and brother-in-law wrote to each other.

Letters?

Why don't you take a look at them?

Wow, what were they about?

My husband, who was an art dealer, and my brother-in-law, who spent 15 years drawing, were exchanging letters discussing artwork.

My husband's name was Theo. My brother-in-law's name was Vincent. Both of them have left this world but...

they had a friendship that was stronger than that of any other two brothers. Vincent was an obscure painter who only sold one piece of art in his whole life.

My husband would always provide his artist brother with money so that he could survive.

What an interesting story!

Jo compiled the letters that Vincent and Theo had written to each other and made a book. The story of the life of a starving artist who followed his passions and never gave up drawing, touched the hearts of many people.

That's amazing. He truly dedicated everything to his art.

How is it that we hadn't heard about this person earlier?

Vincent did not start to become popular until after his death. The exhibit that used his name became very prosperous. Thereafter, the values of Vincent's paintings began to rise at an incredibly fast rate.

Vincent, who had spent his whole life being lonely and wishing that his paintings would sell for more than the cost of the paint, was now the most popular artist in the world.

Wow, it really looks like the stars are pouring down!

It's so intense that I feel like I'm being sucked into the picture.

Van Gogh

The Netherlands and Arles are the two places that are known as "Vincent van Gogh's hometown" and these places are like the Holy Land* for people who love art. The Netherlands is where Vincent was born. Arles is a little village in the South of France that Vincent absolutely loved.

The yellow house that Vincent had stayed in while in Arles, and the many places that could be seen in the background of Vincent's paintings became attractions that many people would try to find.

*Holy Land: A sacred place.

Currently, even just one of his paintings would go for tens of billions of won. Vincent didn't receive the recognition and praise he deserved until after he died. However, in ten years as a painter, he made over 800 oil paintings and left over 1,000 sketches. He was a very passionate painter.

He loved the lives of commoners over the lives of nobility. His pieces of work, in which we can see the world from his eyes, will remain as precious treasures in our world, under the name "Vincent van Gogh."

Word Search

● Find the words which are hidden horizontally, vertically and diagonally.

```
C M Z G Q M Z G Q M Z G Q Q M Z G Q M X
W O I N A E N T I O N H W W N A H C N O
E B M J A B Q J E T E A R B A R I O B M
R V C P R D C K R V V K R R V C K M V M
E C T O A S E N T C A L T T C D U M C E
V X E Q Y N E O Y X N Q Y Y X E N O X M
E Z V W U D I W C Z G W R U Z V J N Z W
A N A E I A E O I A E E E I A R A E A I
L S I R O S G C N S L R H O S G S R S T
P D C U P D H T O D I E O P D H T B D P
A F A Y H F U Y A T C Y V A F U Y I F L
S G S U S T I N C R A G E I N G U T G A
T H S I D H M I D H L I R D H O I Y H U
O J A B S O R A F J T J F F J T J F J S
R K N P R O P O R T I O N A T E B G K I
H L A N H L E N H E E N H H L E N H L B
J Q T M J Q T A U T D O R I T Y M J B L
L W E Q L W Y Q L W Y Q L L W Y Q L U E
Z W R E S E N T Z W K F Z Z S U F T J R
X E M E X M R I N C P O S T U R E X N M
W R Q C C R Q C P R O P H T R Q C C R P
```

pastor	companion	resent	commoner
evangelical	proportionate	posture	plausible

Vocabulary

● Match each word to the correct meaning.

1. struggle	• 무시하다
2. fulfill	• 달성하다
3. masterpiece	• 투쟁하다
4. neglect	• 걸작
5. reliant	• 정신병
6. psychosis	• 의지하는
7. obscure	• 예의상 하는 말
8. recognition	• 귀족
9. missionary	• 무명의
10. courtesy	• 인정
11. aristocrat	• 선교사
12. evaluation	• 평가

Guess What?

- Guess what he said in the blank.

Art Movements

There have been so many styles of art in art history since the Renaissance. Here are the major art movements.

다비드 〈사비니의 여인들〉, 1799년, 루브르 박물관. 고전주의를 대표하는 그림이에요. 인물들이 연극배우처럼 정해진 포즈를 취하고 있는데, 이는 전쟁을 연극의 한 장면처럼 객관화시키려는 화가의 의도입니다.

고야 〈1808년 5월 3일〉, 1814년, 프라도 미술관. 나폴레옹 군대가 스페인을 점령하고 양민들을 잔인하게 처형하는 장면을 그린 걸작이에요.

들라크루아 〈민중을 이끄는 자유의 여신〉, 1830년. 루브르 박물관

Early Renaissance 초기 르네상스
(14th century - 15th century)

High Renaissance 전성기 르네상스
(late 14th century - late 16th century)

Northern Renaissance 북유럽 르네상스
(15th century - 16th century)

Baroque 바로크
(late 16th century - 17th century)

Mannerism 매너리즘
(16th century)

Neo-Classicism 신고전주의
(1750 - 1880)

Romanticism 낭만주의
(18th century - 19th century)

Rococo 로코코
(18th century - 19th century)

르누아르 〈물랭 드 라 갈레트〉, 1876년, 오르세 미술관. 파리의 무도회장 '물랭 드 라 갈레트'의 풍경을 구린 이 작품은 르누아르의 대표적인 인상주의 그림이에요.

쇠라 〈그랑드자트 섬의 일요일 오후〉, 1885년, 시카고 현대 미술관. 인상파 화가 쇠라가 점묘법으로 그린 그림이에요.

고흐 〈론 강의 별이 빛나는 밤〉, 1888년, 오르세 미술관. 고흐는 후기 인상주의 화가입니다.

고흐 〈자화상〉, 1889년, 개인 소장.

Realism 사실주의

(1830 - 1900)

Impressionism 인상주의

(1870 - 1890)

American Impressionism 미국 인상파

(1870 - 1900)

Symbolism 상징주의

(1860 - 1900)

Post Impressionism 후기 인상주의

(1880 - 1910)

Art Nouveau 아르 누보

(1890 - 1914)

Expressionism 표현주의

(1900 - 1920)

Fauvism 야수파

(1900 - 1920)

Cubism 입체파

(1907 - 1920)

Futurism 미래주의

(1907 - 1944)

Constructivism 구성주의

(1917 - 1924)

Dadaism 다다이즘

(1916 - 1950)

Surrealism 초현실주의

(1920 - 1950)

Regionalism 지역주의

(1930 - 1945)

Abstract Expressionism 추상 표현주의

(1945 - 1965)

Pop Art 팝아트

(1955   1975)

Conceptual Art 개념 미술

(1960 onwards)

Media Art 미디어 아트

(1963 onwards)

슈비터스 〈Das Undbild〉, 1919년. 그래픽 디자인, 조각, 그리기 등 다양한 수법을 동원해 완성한 콜라주입니다.

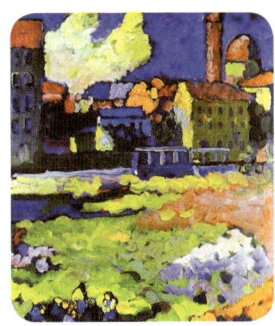

칸딘스키 〈뮌헨 슈바빙의 성 우르술라 교회〉, 1908년. 칸딘스키가 추상주의 화가가 되기 전에 그린 그림이에요.

칸딘스키 〈구성 VII〉, 1913년. 칸딘스키는 추상주의를 대표하는 화가예요.

자코메티의 조각 〈걷는 사람〉, 1961년. 183cm 높이로 제작한 이 작품은 현대인의 나약한 겉모습과 강한 정신을 동시에 표현했다는 평가를 받아요.

연표

1853년   3월 30일, 네덜란드 브라반트 지방의 작은 마을 준데르트에서
6남매의 장남으로 태어났습니다.

1857년 4세   5월 1일, 동생 테오가 태어납니다.

1869년 16세   헤이그에 있는 구필 화랑에 취직합니다.

1873년 20세   구필 화랑 런던 지점으로 직장을 옮깁니다.
하숙집 딸 외제니에게 구혼했다가 거절당합니다.

1875년 22세   파리 지점으로 직장을 옮깁니다.

1876년 23세   근무 태도 불량으로 구필 화랑에서 해고 됩니다.

1877년 24세   목사가 되기 위해 암스테르담으로 갑니다.

1878년 25세   목사가 되는 것을 포기하고 전도사가 되기 위해 보리나주로 갑니다.

1879년 26세   보리나주에서 헌신적으로 마을 사람들을 돌보았지만
성경을 지나치게 글자 그대로 해석했다는 이유로
임시 전도사직에서 해고당합니다.

1880년 27세   화가가 되기로 결심합니다.

1881년 28세   사촌 매형 모베의 지도로 그림을 배우기 시작합니다.

1883년	30세	고향으로 돌아와 그림을 그리는데 매진합니다.
1885년	32세	〈감자먹는 사람들〉을 그립니다.
		안트베르펜으로 가서 미술 학원에 등록합니다.
		일본 민속 판화 우키요에를 알게 됩니다.
1886년	33세	파리로 가서 테오와 함께 지냅니다.
1887년	34세	고갱, 쇠라, 시냐크, 피사로 등 인상파 화가들과 사귀면서 영향을 받습니다.
1888년	35세	아를로 떠나 작품에 매진합니다.
		10월, 고갱과 함께 생활하기 시작합니다.
		12월, 고갱이 고흐를 떠납니다.
1889년	36세	환각 증상을 일으켜 아를을 떠납니다.
		5월, 정신 병원에 입원하여 작품 활동을 계속합니다.
1890년	37세	1월, 붉은 포도밭이 400프랑에 팔렸습니다.
		5월, 의사인 가셰와 친분을 쌓습니다.
		7월 27일, 권총 자살을 시도했습니다.
		7월 29일, 세상을 떠납니다.
1891년		1월, 테오가 정신 착란을 일으키다가 사망합니다.

Note